by Mike Dion   illustrated by Barbara Maslen

MODERN CURRICULUM PRESS
Pearson Learning Group

Jake's older sister, Tina, had resolved to open her own business when she graduated from college. Then just as she was looking for the right business to buy, Rosie's Flower Shop came up for sale. The great thing about it was that her Aunt Rose had started the shop years ago. Aunt Rose had sold the shop five years before. And now that owner was selling. Tina had saved her money, Aunt Rose had helped out a little, and now it would become the new and improved Rosie's Flower Shop!

"I want to open in two weeks," said Tina with a smile. " I should be able to do it. I've already ordered flowers."

Jake believed she could do it. Tina was very efficient. She had already painted the walls and put in a new cooler for cut flowers. She'd also put up glass shelves. Except for the plants and flowers, the front room was ready for business.

But the back room was a mess. Dusty boxes crowded the space. The room was filled with old baskets and vases of all kinds. Tina needed to clear the worktable and clean the sink. She needed the space for new vases and baskets. Jake resolved to help her.

A rusted flower cart took up most of the space in the back room. Jake maneuvered his way around it.

He walked over to a small pile of cartons that had just been delivered to the shop. They were filled with new vases Tina had ordered for the store. Jake pulled a vase from a carton and set it on a shelf.

He pulled out another vase a little too fast. The vase hit the floor and shattered. Jake groaned. Tina would not be pleased.

Tina peered into the back room.

"Jake!" she said. "What happened?"

"Sorry, Tina," said Jake. "I took out a new vase, and I dropped it."

"It broke?" asked Tina.

"It shattered."

Tina sighed. Starting a new business was risky and expensive. She couldn't afford to have things smashed before she even opened.

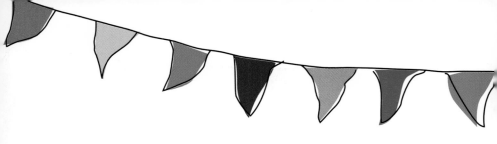

"Please don't handle any more of them. Okay, Jake?" she asked. "I'm not ready to put new things out yet. First I have to clear away the old ones. And I need to clean and paint the shelves."

"I apologize," said Jake.

"I'll tell you what," said Tina. "I'll do the painting and put out the new items. You can help in other ways."

Like sweeping, Jake thought. He got out the broom and dustpan.

"Like how?" he asked.

"We need to spread the news that the shop is going to reopen," said Tina. "We also need to get rid of all this old junk. Do you think you can find a way to do that?"

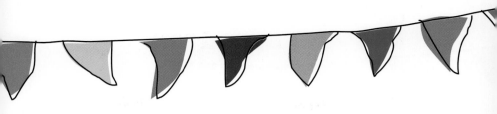

"I don't know," said Jake. "I'd rather paint."

"Jake," said Tina. "You'd probably just drip paint all over the floor."

She was right. The last time he'd painted that's just what had happened. Jake swept up the glass bits. Then he looked at the junk all around him. Cleaning it out was too big a job for one person. Of course, the spreading-the-news part was a huge job too. He decided he'd better call in Grady and Ben.

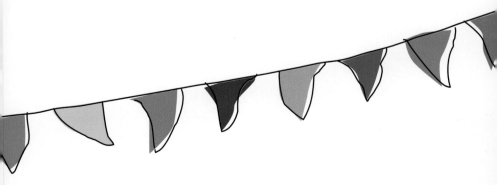

Grady and Ben were Jake's best friends. Ben would help with any task, as long as you fed him. Grady got a new idea every minute. Jake was sure he'd think of a good way to let people know about Tina's new business. The only thing Jake could think of was to advertise in the paper. But Tina the Efficient had already done that. Every day an ad on page nine of the news read:

Rosie's Flower Shop

Come to the Grand Reopening!

We'll make your life beautiful.

25 Shadyside Road

Jake convinced his friends to come to the flower shop by promising to get them pizza.

"Tina needs our help," said Jake. "How should we let people know about the reopening of the shop? What's a good advertising plan? And how can we get rid of all the useless stuff in the back room?"

"Food first," said Ben, "then we'll think." He took
the biggest piece of pizza and smacked his lips. Then he
reached for another slice.

"What about getting a flower cart to put outside
the store?" said Grady.

"Actually, we already have one," said Jake.

Jake brought them into the back room. He pointed to the iron flower cart. The cart was once white. Now it was mostly just rust. The two giant iron wheels used to roll. Now they were stuck tight. One of the two long handles on the cart was loose. It was not a pretty sight.

"That would make a great go-cart!" said Ben.

"Let's fix it up," said Grady.

"And make it into a go-cart?" said Jake. "Paint 'Rosie's Flower Shop' on the side as an ad?"

"Yeah!" said Ben.

"No, I meant let's fix it so Tina can set it out in front of the shop," said Grady. "It will look pretty, and get people's attention."

"Well, your idea makes more sense than mine," said Ben, "but it isn't as much fun."

"Tina can put flowers and plants in it," said Grady. "It will draw people right into the shop."

Grady and Ben began to root around the room, examining the boxes and shelves.

"Hey, Jake!" shouted Ben. "I thought you said all this was useless junk."

"It is," replied Jake. "Just look at it."

"Well, I'm looking," said Ben, "and I'm telling you that most of this stuff is not junk."

Ben pointed to a box filled with a rusty heap of what looked like scrap metal. "These are old gardening tools. They don't make them like this any more. People love to buy old things like these tools."

Grady opened another box and pulled out a bronze vase. It was tarnished, but still looked beautiful. "Hey," he said. "Why don't we clean up these things and sell them? We could display them on the flower cart and hold a sale to advertise the opening of the flower shop!"

Tina liked their idea. She said she'd pay for supplies, and she told them they could keep half the money they made on selling the stuff from the back room.

The boys got to work on the cart quickly. They oiled the wheels. They sanded the rusty spots. They tightened the handles with new screws. Then they cleaned the whole cart and painted it green. When they were done with the cart, they started working on the old gardening tools and vases.

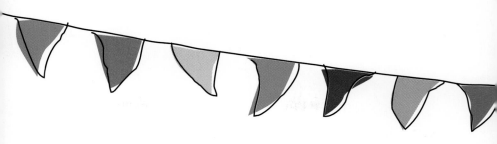

"Not bad," said Grady when they were finished. "Not bad at all."

"It's better than not bad," said Ben. "It's great!"

The boys maneuvered the cart outside to see how it looked in the sunlight. Even when the cart was empty, Tina loved it. They decided to hold the flower cart sale to sell the old stuff on the following Saturday. That would be one week before the flower shop reopened.

"We'll wheel the cart out in front of the shop and have the sale right there," said Jake. "When people come to the flower cart sale, they'll see signs about the opening of Rosie's Flower Shop next week."

"But how are you going to get people to the flower cart sale?" asked Tina.

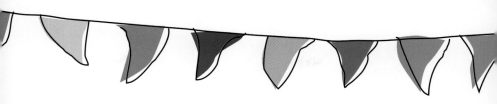

"Signs," said Jake. "Everyone in this town tapes signs to the street lamps—signs for concerts, signs for lost puppies. We'll tape up flower cart sale signs."

"Right," said Tina. "Everyone makes signs. That's the problem. We need something new."

Jake looked at a box of old faded ribbon. He picked up a wide yellow spool.

"We could make signs on the wide ribbons!" he said.

"Yeah!" said Grady. He held up a silk flower. "And stick these on the ribbon banners!"

"And tie the banners to the lamp posts!" said Ben.

"And not just downtown," said Jake. "We can tie them to street lamps all over!"

The ribbon banners were up. And they looked great. Early on Saturday morning, Jake, Grady, and Ben maneuvered the flower cart outside the shop. They set it up right in front of the front door. Jake and Ben heaped the cart with all of the objects from the back room. Grady painted a sign right on the front window. It said, "Rosie's Flower Shop! Grand Opening Next Saturday!"

The first shoppers appeared before they were even finished setting up.

"This is going to be great! " Said Jake.

Tina smiled in agreement.

Every time the boys sold something, they gave the buyer a silk flower with a ribbon that advertised the new flower shop. Grady tied more flower banners to the trees in front of the shop. Ben gave more silk flowers to little kids, who waved them around to watch the ribbons flutter.

"They're little walking ads!" said Ben.

"They're perfect," said Tina.

By the end of the day, the boys had sold most of the old things. They packed up what was left to bring to the thrift shop. Then they took down all the banners they had put up. Last of all they brought the flower cart back inside.

Tina had the back room cleaned up and painted.

"I'll heap the cart with flowers and plants next weekend!" said Tina. "It will look beautiful! Aunt Rose is coming to the opening. She will be so pleased to see the shop open and looking good again."

"Ice cream time!" said Ben.

Tina laughed. "Thank you for all your help," she said. "I hope you can come to the opening too!"

Jake got to the shop early the day of the opening. The shop looked great. But when it opened, no one was there except Tina, Jake, and Aunt Rose. Jake's high hopes were shattered. He didn't know what to say.

"Where are the customers?" asked Aunt Rose.

Jake resolved to help out again. He gave Grady and Ben a call.

"No one's at Rosie's Flower Shop!" he said.

"Do you know why?" asked Grady. "There's a brand new department store opening in the center of town! Everyone has gone there instead!"

This was horrible news. Poor Tina! She'd worked so hard!

"What can we do?" asked Jake.

"I'll get Ben and we'll come over," said Grady. "We'll think of something."

Jake couldn't stand to be inside the shop with all its beautiful flowers and plants, and no customers. He went outside and stood by the flower cart. The cart looked great filled with flowers. Jake pulled on the handles. The cart was heavy, but it rolled forward smoothly. Then he rolled it back.

Ben and Grady wheeled up on their bicycles.

"Sorry it took so long," said Ben. "Downtown is crowded!"

"You should see the people in front of that new department store!" said Grady.

"Rosie's Flower Shop should be downtown too," said Jake, "instead of on a quiet side street."

"It's a shame the shop isn't on wheels," joked Ben. "We could drive it down where all the people are."

That gave Jake an idea.

"The flower cart is on wheels!" he said. "Why don't we just roll it downtown? We'll introduce all those people to Rosie's Flower Shop!"

He went inside to ask Tina if it was okay.

"It sounds a little crazy," she said. "But maybe it will work. Poor Aunt Rose is so upset!"

So was Tina. Jake could see that. Her jaw was clenched, the way it got when she was worried. He remembered that there were still some flower banners left over from last week's sale. Yes, there they were, in a plastic bucket underneath the work table.

Jake brought the flower banners out to the cart.
He and Grady and Ben stuck them into the vases and
potted plants. Then they pulled the flower cart down
to the center of town.

The boys rolled the cart up and down Main Street.
They handed out flower banners.

"Buy flowers at Rosie's Flower Shop!" they called.

They maneuvered the cart through the crowds
outside the new department store. By the time they
got back to the shop, a few people were following
them. By the end of the day, the boys had pulled the
flower cart through the middle of town three times.
Each time people followed them back to the shop.
Each time Tina sold more flowers.

Tina's opening day wasn't as big as she'd hoped it would be. But she wasn't too disappointed.

"Well it was a good day after all," she said. "No matter how efficient you are, there are some things you just can't predict."

"Like when other stores open," said Jake.

"Or what a great help you'd be!" said Tina. She gave Jake a big hug.

"I was glad to help," Jake squeaked.

"Me too," said Grady.

"If you want, you can say thank you with a sandwich," laughed Ben.

⊙ Comprehension Skill: Making Judgments

Modern Curriculum Press edition, 2004

ISBN 0-7652-3504-8

Printed in the United States of America

1 2 3 4 5 6 7 8 9 10   08 07 06 05 04 03

Pearson Learning Group

1-800-321-3106
www.pearsonlearning.com

A Grand Opening

Power Reader #58

**Comprehension Skill:
Making Judgments**

Genre: Realistic Story

DRA® Level	50
Guided Reading Level	S
Lexile® Measure	490L

1-800-321-3106
www.pearsonlearning.com

**Modern
Curriculum
Press**

Pearson Learning Group

ISBN 0-7652-3504-8

90000

9 780765 235046

Disaster
Super Heroes
The Red Cross

by Phoebe Marsh